DISCOVER!

PEOPLE of the PAST

WHO WAS GEORGE WASHINGTON?

Robert Clore

Enslow PUBLISHING

Please visit our website, www.enslow.com. For a free color catalog of all our high-quality books, call toll free 1-800-398-2504 or fax 1-877-980-4454.

Cataloging-in-Publication Data
Names: Clore, Robert.
Title: Who was George Washington? / Robert Clore.
Description: Buffalo, NY : Enslow Publishing, 2027. | Series: People of the past | Includes glossary.
Identifiers: ISBN 9781978550506 (pbk.) | ISBN 9781978550513 (library bound) | ISBN 9781978550520 (ebook)
Subjects: LCSH: Washington, George, 1732-1799–Juvenile literature. | Presidents–United States–Juvenile literature. | United States–History–Revolution, 1775-1783–Biography–Juvenile literature.
Classification: LCC E312.66 C657 2027 | DDC 973.41092 B–dc23

Published in 2027 by
Enslow Publishing
2544 Clinton Street
Buffalo, NY 14224

Designer: Claire Vanden Branden
Editor: Max Pritchard

Photo Credits: Cover, p. 1 Rawpixel.com/Shutterstock.com; p. 5 Smithsonian Institution; pp. 7, 19 Library of Congress; pp. 9, 11 Wikimedia Commons; p. 13 The Metropolitan Museum of Art; p. 15 Architect of the Capitol; p. 17 National Archives; p. 21 Sean Pavone/Shutterstock.com.

Printed in China

CPSIA compliance information: Batch #QS27ENS: For further information contact Enslow Publishing, at 1-800-398-2504.

CONTENTS

BOLDFACE WORDS APPEAR IN THE GLOSSARY.

AN IMPORTANT LEADER

George Washington served as the first president of the United States. He led the **colonial** army during the **American Revolution**. He played an important role in founding the young country and keeping it together.

CHILDHOOD AND EARLY ADULTHOOD

George was born in 1732 to a wealthy Virginia family. His father died when George was 11. George spent lots of time with his oldest brother at the family home, which was called Mount Vernon. After his brother died, George became the owner of Mount Vernon at 20 years old. He managed the farm and its enslaved people.

Virginia was one of 13 colonies under British rule in what is now the United States. In 1752, George joined the Virginia **militia**. He was an **officer** during a war between France and England that began in 1754. George became well respected. In 1759, he married Martha Dandridge Custis. They lived at Mount Vernon.

THE REVOLUTIONARY WAR

By the 1760s, the 13 colonies were unhappy with British rule. In 1774, **representatives** from all the colonies met in Philadelphia, Pennsylvania. George represented Virginia. He shared his views on many matters.

The American Revolution began in 1775. George was chosen to lead the colonial army. He kept the colonial army going despite heavy losses and low resources. George's leadership helped the colonists win the war in 1783. The colonies could now form an independent nation, the United States of America.

A NEW NATION

George returned to Philadelphia in 1787. There, he was part of the group that met to write the **US Constitution**. The Constitution stated that the people would cast votes for the country's leader, the president.

A POPULAR PRESIDENT

George was chosen as the first US president in 1789. Most states only allowed white, landowning men to vote. In his first term, George supported the Bill of **Rights**. This list of rights became part of the Constitution. It protected freedom of religion, freedom of speech, and many more rights.

Congress of the United States,
begun and held at the City of New-York, on
Wednesday the fourth of March, one thousand seven hundred and eighty nine.

THE BILL OF RIGHTS

George was so well liked that he was voted into office again in 1792. **Political parties** were beginning to form. George did not like how divided politics was becoming. Meanwhile, he kept the United States out of wars between European countries. He chose to step down after two terms in office, returning to Mount Vernon.

GEORGE'S LEGACY

George died on December 14, 1799. People across the world honored him. Washington, DC, and the state of Washington are named for him. The Washington Monument was built in honor of him. His birthday is celebrated on the third Monday every February. This holiday is sometimes known as Presidents' Day.

GLOSSARY

American Revolution: The war in which the American colonies won their freedom from England.

colonial: Having to do with colonies, which are lands under the control of another country.

militia: A group of people who only fight when needed.

officer: Somebody who commands a military force.

political parties: Groups of people with the same goals working to win elections and make laws.

representatives: People who stand for a group of people.

rights: Freedoms that are protected by law.

US Constitution: The piece of writing that states the laws of the United States.

FOR MORE INFORMATION

Books

Britton, Tamara L. *George Washington*. Minneapolis, MN: Abdo Publishing, 2025.

Murray, Stuart. *American Revolution*. New York, NY: DK, 2022.

Websites

Britannica Kids: George Washington
kids.britannica.com/kids/article/George-Washington/345536
Read and watch a video about Washington's life and check out historical images.

George Washington
kids.nationalgeographic.com/history/article/george-washington
Read about the different stages of George Washington's life.

Publisher's note to educators and parents: Our editors have carefully reviewed these websites to ensure that they are suitable for students. Many websites change frequently, however, and we cannot guarantee that a site's future contents will continue to meet our high standards of quality and educational value. Be advised that students should be closely supervised whenever they access the internet.

INDEX